WORKING ANIMALS

Farming

WORKING ANIMALS

Farming

Claudia Martin

Marshall Cavendish
Benchmark
New York

Other Marshall Cavendish Offices:
Marshall Cavendish International (Asia) Private Limited, 1 New Industrial Road, Singapore 536196 • Marshall Cavendish International (Thailand) Co Ltd. 253 Asoke, 12th Flr, Sukhumvit 21 Road, Klongtoey Nua, Wattana, Bangkok 10110, Thailand • Marshall Cavendish (Malaysia) Sdn Bhd, Times Subang, Lot 46, Subang Hi-Tech Industrial Park, Batu Tiga, 40000 Shah Alam, Selangor Darul Ehsan, Malaysia

Marshall Cavendish is a trademark of Times Publishing Limited

All websites were available and accurate when this book was sent to press.

Library of Congress Cataloging-in-Publication Data

Martin, Claudia.
  Farming / Claudia Martin. – 1st ed.
      p. cm. – (Working animals)
  Includes index.
  Summary: "Describes animals that work on farms and ranches in various ways: herding cattle and sheep, pulling machinery, and providing products such as eggs, milk, leather, and wool"–Provided by publisher.
  ISBN 978-1-60870-162-9
  1. Agriculture–Juvenile literature. 2. Working animals–Juvenile literature. I. Title.
  S519.M37 2010
  636–dc22
                              2010006895

Editorial and design by
Amber Books Ltd
Bradley's Close
74–77 White Lion Street
London N1 9PF
United Kingdom
www.amberbooks.co.uk

Project Editor: James Bennett
Copy Editor: Peter Mavrikis
Design: Andrew Easton
Picture Research: Terry Forshaw, Natascha Spargo

Printed in China
135642

CONTENTS

Chapter 1
The Herders

Around the world, animals work alongside farmers, helping them to look after their herds. A farmer's herd needs to be fed, moved from place to place, and protected from predators. Animals such as dogs and horses can help with all of these tasks.

Herding Dogs

Herding dogs are trained to both lead and gather animals such as sheep, cattle, horses, goats, deer, and even chickens. The animals are herded, or "mustered," when a farmer wants to move them to a different location, feed them, provide them with medical treatment, or transport them for sale. Herding dogs usually belong to a **breed** that has been developed over many generations to make good herders. For example, the German shepherd dog has been bred to have

◄ **An Australian kelpie sheepdog watches over its flock.**

▲ **Herding dogs work with animals from pigs to turkeys.**

the speed, intelligence, and obedience needed for herding sheep. The tiny Cardigan and Pembroke Welsh corgis have been used in Wales for hundreds of years to herd cows, horses, and sheep. They were bred to nip at the animals' heels to move them along. Since these dogs are short, any kicks from the animals being herded pass over their heads, so they are not injured. Dogs that use these tactics are known as "heelers." Other breeds work in front of the herd, staring the animals down to make them obey. These dogs, such as the Border collie, are known as "headers."

▼ **Border collies were bred in Northumberland, near the border between Scotland and England. Today, they work with farmers around the world.**

Ancient Herding Dogs

Many breeds compete for the title of most ancient herding dog. One possible winner is the Rottweiler. It is thought that this breed dates back to the time of the Roman Empire, nearly two thousand years ago, when Roman lands stretched from North Africa to northern Europe. The Roman army traveled with its meat supplies on the hoof—they moved their cattle from place to place, and needed the help of dogs to keep the herds in order. The Rottweiler is named after the German town of Rottweil, which was founded by the Romans in the first century C.E. The dogs are thought to be the descendants of local dogs as well as dogs the Romans brought with them. The Rottweil area later became an important cattle-farming region, and the Rottweilers left behind by the Romans proved their worth as herders and **livestock** guardians.

Rottweilers still herd livestock all over the world, but they also serve in roles from guard dogs to guide dogs for the blind. The Rottweiler's intelligence and loyalty have led to its becoming one of the most popular breeds in the United States. This dog has something of a bad reputation for having a temper and being more likely than some other breeds to attack humans. In fact, attacks are nearly always caused by owners not giving these large, strong dogs the proper care and training that they need.

▲ **As well as working at herding and guarding livestock, Rottweilers were once also used as draft dogs, pulling carts loaded with meat to the local market.**

"All dogs have a natural instinct to chase animals such as sheep and goats, which at one time would have been their natural prey."

Herding dogs respond to a farmer's whistles, hand movements, and voice commands. All dogs have a natural **instinct** to chase animals such as sheep and goats, which at one time would have been their natural **prey**. With herding dogs, this instinct is matched with a high level of training that allows them to control the herd without causing any

▼ **Herding dogs need to be intelligent and obedient.**

▶ **The Great Pyrenees dog was bred to protect sheep from wolves and bears.**

harm. Herding dogs are introduced to the herd at a young age and encouraged to behave calmly around the animals. Their training involves being praised and rewarded for mastering each task, such as circling the herd or rounding up a stray animal. It can take several years before a dog masters all the skills needed to be a good herder.

Guardians of the Herd

Some farming dogs are trained not to herd but to guard a farmer's livestock. These guardian dogs protect the animals from **predators**, such as wolves, coyotes, and even cheetahs and lions. They keep an eye open for threats. Guardian dogs are often used to protect flocks of sheep, but farmers may also employ them to watch over

▼ **Livestock guardian dogs, such as the Akbash, are known for their loyalty to their herd. The Akbash enjoys sitting or lying among its flock of sheep.**

Livestock Guardians around the World

Guardian dogs can usually be found wherever livestock is at risk from predators. Here are some examples of breeds used around the world:

- In Namibia, Africa, Anatolian dogs guard herds of goats from cheetahs.
- In Tibet, the Tibetan mastiff protects yaks, sheep, and goats from predators as large as leopards.
- In the American West, large breeds such as the komondor, Great Pyrenees, and Akbash, protect sheep from coyotes.
- In Australia, Maremma sheepdogs are being trained to protect penguins on Middle Island, off the country's southern coast, from predators such as foxes.

▲ **Cheetah conservation groups have donated Anatolian shepherd dogs to goat farmers in Namibia. The dogs scare away the cheetahs so that farmers do not have to shoot the endangered cats.**

> **❝A guardian dog is introduced to its herd while it's still a young puppy, perhaps as young as three weeks of age.❞**

cattle, goats, llamas, and other animals. The dogs chosen to be livestock guardians are usually large and always very protective by nature.

A guardian dog is introduced to its herd while it's still a young puppy, perhaps as young as three weeks of age. This is so the dog can become familiar with the animals' smell and gradually grow attached to them so that a long-lasting bond forms. A dog will be protective of members of another species only when it has been brought up with them. A dog raised to take care of goats will usually not be a good guardian if it has to look after sheep instead.

Just one dog or several dogs may look after a herd, depending on the size of the herd and the risk from predators. Where a group of dogs is used, often the dogs will take different roles. Some will stay among the herd in case of an attack, while others will patrol at the herd's edges to keep predators at a distance.

If a predator is spotted, the dogs can usually drive it away with a display of aggressiveness and loud barking and growling. Livestock guardians hardly ever actually kill predators, as their presence alone is enough to ward off attacks. This makes guardian dogs popular with wildlife **conservationists**, who are eager to protect predators such as the world's remaining wolves, coyotes, and cheetahs.

Working with Cowboys and Cowgirls

On cattle and sheep ranches in the West, horses are often the best herders. They work with the cowboys and cowgirls who look after the animals. Traveling on horseback is, even today, the best way to herd the animals, since they roam on huge expanses of land. Herding horses don't work only in the West. They can also be found on ranches in South America and Australia.

Camargue Horses

One of the most famous and beautiful breeds of horse used by cowboys is the Camargue of southern France. These horses are ridden by the traditional cowboys of the Camargue region, known as *gardians*. The *gardians* look after the black Camargue cattle that live semi-wild in the marshes. The bulls in the herds are regularly rounded up and used in the sport of bullfighting. In Camargue-style bullfighting, the bull is not killed. Instead, each bullfighter is given fifteen minutes to capture ribbons that have been tied to the bull's horns.

The Camargue horses are an ancient breed that lives mostly wild in the wetlands of the Rhone River delta. The breed was admired by the ancient Romans when they conquered the Camargue some two thousand years ago. Camargue horses are known for their intelligence, strength, and agility. All of the adult horses are gray, but they are born with a black or dark brown coat that slowly fades. Although most of the horses still live wild, grazing on grasses, the horses ridden by the *gardians* are **domesticated** and highly trained. Camargue horses also often take part in sporting events and competitions around the world.

▲ A *gardian* **rounds up a herd of wild Camargue horses, famous for their beauty, strength, and intelligence.**

The horses that work on ranches, often called stock horses, need to be tough, brave, and calm. In many cases, they belong to particular breeds that have been developed over generations to have the right characteristics. In the United States, many stock horses belong to the American quarter horse breed, which was developed mainly in Texas. In Australia, a breed known as the Australian stock horse is often used. The breed's ancestors date back to the earliest horses brought to Australia by European settlers, in the late 1700s.

Stock horses also need to be intelligent. Since a cowboy or cowgirl will often require one hand free for performing various tasks, the horse must need only light touches on its reins to tell it where to go. It should also have what is known as "cow sense"—a natural understanding of the behavior of cattle. A horse with good cow sense will know just where to position

◄ A cowboy uses a rope, known as a lariat, to catch a horse.

Herding Dog Commands

The commands given to herding dogs vary around the world, but some of them are likely to be:
- "Cast" – Gather the herd into a group.
- "Hold" – Keep the herd where it is.
- "Bark" or "Speak up" – Bark at the herd to make the animals obey.
- "Look back" – Find a stray animal.
- "That'll do" – Return to the farmer.

▲ Dogs obey the command to "look back" and find a stray calf.

❝A horse that is well trained in cutting will be able to keep the animal separate from the herd with little or no help from the rider.❞

itself for its rider to carry out any particular job.

Horses perform a variety of tasks on a ranch. A cow or bull may need to be lassoed, or caught. A horse whose rider is roping cattle in this way must be strong in order to pull against the weight of the heavy animal. Sometimes one animal will need to be drawn away from the rest, perhaps to be vaccinated or sold. This task is called "cutting." A horse that is well trained in cutting will be able to keep the animal separate from the herd with little or no help from the rider.

▼ **Cowboys and cowgirls are at work in many countries where livestock is kept on open land, such as in Patagonia, Argentina.**

The Real Cowboys

Everyone knows about cowboys and the nineteenth-century Wild West from the movies—or thinks that they do. But what's the real story? The earliest cowboys started work in the Americas in the sixteenth century, when Spanish settlers shipped over their horses and domesticated cattle. In the second half of the nineteenth century, the American cattle industry rapidly expanded. Many men traveled to the West to find work on the vast ranches. They were from many different backgrounds, but one thing they all had in common was that they were poor and did a hard day's work. Cowgirls worked alongside the men, particularly on small, family-owned farms where everyone had to help out.

▲ **Cowboys have always just been hard-working ranch hands, even though the movies tell us that they were gun-fighting outlaws.**

Chapter 2
Animals with Pull

Some animals work on farms as draft animals. They are valued for their strength and are used for pulling farm machinery or carting newly harvested crops. Draft animals range from horses and donkeys to camels, oxen, reindeer, and water buffalo.

Draft Horses

Until about sixty years ago, draft horses were commonly found on farms throughout North America and Europe. They could often be seen dragging plows and pulling cartloads of crops. With the increased use of motorized vehicles, particularly the tractor, the need for draft horses in North America and Europe has nearly died out. In other areas of the world, however, where motorized transportation is too costly, draft horses are still working hard. And even in some parts of the United States and western Europe, draft horses continue to be favored by farmers who prefer a source of power that doesn't need fuel.

◄ **Clydesdale draft horses pull an old-fashioned plow.**

▲ **A reindeer team hauls a sleigh in Siberia, Russia.**

Where Can We See Draft Horses?

Although draft horses are no longer commonly used on farms in North America and western Europe, draft horse breeds—such as huge, muscled Shire horses and Clydesdales—have not completely died out. If you would like to see draft horses at work, agricultural museums that re-enact the farming methods of the past are good places to see them pull plows and carts. Draft horses can also be seen displaying their skills and competing in contests at agricultural shows. In England, Shire horses are kept by one or two traditional breweries (where beer is made) to transport beer to pubs. And the strength and good nature of draft horses have made some breeds popular pets, which owners ride for pleasure and enter into competitions.

▲ **In some places draft horses can still be seen hard at work on farms.**

After horses were domesticated, different breeds were developed to do different jobs. All draft horse breeds are tall and muscular. They have strong shoulders and hindquarters so that they can pull with great power. A member of the breed of draft horse known as the Shire horse is the tallest horse on record, standing at 7 feet 2½ inches (2.2 meters) tall.

Draft Animals around the World

While machines have replaced animals in the industrialized world, many farmers in less developed countries still rely on animal power.

▼ The Suffolk Punch is an English draft horse breed known for its great strength. It is still occasionally employed in forestry work.

"*Since water buffalo live naturally in wetlands and swamps, they are well suited to plowing paddy fields, the flooded sections of land where rice is grown.*"

A farmer's choice of animal depends on the tasks to be performed and the animals available in the region.

The water buffalo is a large type of cattle that is native to Asia. It is widely used as a draft animal there, as well as in North Africa. In Southeast Asia, the water buffalo provides about 25 percent of the farm power. Since water buffalo live naturally in wetlands and swamps, they are well suited to plowing paddy

▼ **In Thailand, many farmers cannot afford mechanized plows, so they rely on water buffalo to plow their paddy fields.**

Hairy Yaks!

High in the Himalayan mountains of Asia, farmers have to rely on a very hairy and sure-footed draft animal: the yak. The yak is a hoofed mammal, related to cows. It has long, shaggy hair, which helps it to endure the cold of this icy region. The yak is kept by many farmers in places such as Nepal, Tibet, and Mongolia. As well as being used for pulling plows and carrying loads on its back, the yak offers many other resources. On the high Tibetan plateau, where trees are unable to grow because of the cold, yak dung is often the only fuel available to burn. Yaks are also kept for their meat and provide wool for clothing. Yak milk can be turned into a cheese and is also used in a special tea, called *po cha*, which contains tea leaves, yak butter, and salt. A Tibetan farmer might drink several bowls of *po cha* before work in the morning, as it gives plenty of energy and the butter prevents chapped lips from the wind and sun. Yak butter is also used to fuel lamps.

▲ **In Mongolia, a yak pulls an agricultural load. Besides providing wool, fuel, and milk, the yak is a source of food. Its meat is often dried, so that it can be carried around easily by herders.**

fields, the flooded sections of land where rice is grown. Rice is the key crop in much of Asia. Water buffalo can also provide meat and milk, while their dung can be used as both fuel and fertilizer.

Oxen are used around the world—particularly in Africa, Asia, and South America— for a range of farming tasks. Oxen are not a special breed of cattle. The term oxen refers to any large kind of cattle that has been trained as a draft animal. In addition to plowing, oxen are also used for hauling wagons, powering farming equipment, and grinding grain by trampling on it or by driving machines that crush it. Oxen can pull harder than horses, although they are not as fast. A trained ox can respond to a range of voice commands from its driver.

▼ **Oxen are widely used for farming in Africa.**

Draft Animal Welfare

In the developing world, food, water, and resources can be scarce for both humans and animals. In such an environment, draft animals are often overworked and malnourished. Sometimes they don't get enough water and become dehydrated. Children are often responsible for the care of a family's draft animal, but they might not recognize the signs of illness. Even when an animal is discovered to be sick, the family may not be able to afford medical care. Many developing nations do not have animal welfare organizations, but there are groups at work worldwide that educate farmers about animal care and provide assistance.

▲ **Hardworking draft animals need a great deal of care and attention.**

« Mules are considered to be better workers than horses because they need less food and can carry more weight than horses of a similar size. »

Camels, elephants, donkeys, and mules are just some of the other animals that are at work in different countries, carrying goods on their backs or dragging farm equipment. Mules are the offspring of a male donkey and a female horse. They are considered to be better workers than horses because they need less food and can carry more weight than horses of a similar size. The largest draft animals are elephants, which are used in parts of Asia to haul the heaviest loads, such as logs.

▼ **Some people think mules are cleverer than either horses or donkeys.**

▶ **Elephants are employed in Myanmar to drag heavy teakwood logs.**

Chapter 3
The Producers

Some farm animals are kept as livestock for the products they provide. They are the "producers." Their products range from food, such as meat, eggs, milk, and honey, to fibers, which become fabrics such as wool and silk.

Giving Us Food

The most common livestock animals are cows, sheep, chickens, and pigs. These four kinds of animals supply most of the meat that we eat. Chickens also produce eggs, while cows and sheep make milk.

Other livestock animals that are raised for their meat include camels, deer, guinea pigs, llamas, turkeys, and yaks. Goats, like cows and sheep, produce both milk and meat. In addition, the dung of many livestock animals can be used as

◀ **Bees have been kept for their honey for thousands of years.**

▲ **Cattle provide milk, meat, leather, and fertilizer.**

Working Insects

Insects are probably the hardest-working animals of all. Everyone knows about the giant cities that tiny termites build and the millions of flowers that flying insects pollinate every year. Some insects are also busily at work on products that we use every day. Bees have been kept in

▲ **Silkworms eat white mulberry or osage-orange leaves.**

human-built hives for thousands of years so that the honey and honeycomb they produce can be collected. Silkworms have been farmed for at least five thousand years. These creatures build a cocoon made of silk thread, which can be woven into a soft and valuable cloth.

▲ **Silkworms are the larvae of silkmoths. When the larvae are mature, they enclose themselves in a cocoon of raw silk. Each cocoon is made of up to 3,000 feet (900 meters) of thread.**

fertilizer to help grow crops. It can also be burned as a fuel.

Farming is not limited to the land. Fish farming is practiced around the world. Rather than going through the effort and expense of catching fish in oceans, seas, and rivers, some people breed fish such as salmon, carp, catfish, and sturgeon on fish farms. In addition to the fish meat, the eggs of some fish species are considered to be a great delicacy. The eggs of the sturgeon are called caviar and can cost as much as $1,600 a pound!

Wool and Leather

Many of our clothes are made from **fibers** that are produced by

▼ Sheep's wool is used for clothing, rugs, and house insulation. Lanolin, a waxy fat extracted from wool, is used in cosmetics.

❝Leather is made by tanning the skins of dead animals such as cows or deer. Tanning turns the skin into a long-lasting fabric that is used for products from shoes to coats.❞

animals. Some animals, such as sheep, goats, and alpacas, can be shorn for their **fleece** without being harmed. The wool or fur is then spun and woven to produce cloth. Particular breeds of rabbit, such as the angora, are also shorn for their soft and thick hair.

Leather is made by tanning the skins of dead animals such as cows or deer. Tanning turns the skin into a long-lasting fabric that is used for products from shoes to coats. Reptiles such as crocodiles, alligators, and snakes are also farmed for their skins, which are popular among some people for boots, belts, and handbags. However, many people—including vegans, who will not use animal products for food or clothing—are against the use of leather.

"No" to Fur Farming?

When used in clothing, fur is animal skin with the hair left on for warmth and softness. In order to obtain the fur, the animals must be killed. Animals farmed for their fur include minks, rabbits, foxes, and chinchillas. Many people oppose killing animals for their fur. And even though they may wear leather, a lot of people do not like the idea of wearing the skin of an animal that has not been killed for its meat. Fur farming is banned in the United Kingdom, Austria, and Croatia.

◀ **An angora rabbit is first shorn or gently plucked for its hair. Then the hair is spun into long, soft threads.**

Farming Practices

Some farmers raise just one or two kinds of animals in order to feed their own family. This is often the case in the developing world. But in places such as the United States and western Europe, animals are often raised on large farms that keep just one type of animal, such as cows, pigs or chickens. Many farmers use machinery, such as milking machines, that makes their work quicker and easier. These farming practices can increase a farmer's profit without distressing the animals or affecting the quality of the food produced.

However, many animals raised in the United States and Europe are now being "factory farmed." This means that a high number of animals are raised in a fairly small area. The animals are often kept indoors, rather

▲ Milking machines, which do not harm the cows, are commonly used on dairy farms.

▶ Closely confined "factory-farmed" chickens are a cause of concern, both for the chickens and the humans who eat them.

« In many countries, laws govern the treatment of all farm animals and the way in which food is produced. »

than being allowed to roam free. This reduces a farmer's costs, since land—as well as employing people to look after the animals—can be expensive.

Animal welfare groups and many farmers are concerned that factory-farmed animals often live in cramped and distressing conditions. Disease can spread fast among these closely confined animals. Also, there is concern about the artificial methods sometimes used on the animals. Some farmers give their livestock vitamin supplements. Some use **hormones** to make the animals grow bigger.

It's Up to You

It is up to **consumers** to decide how they would like their meat, milk, and eggs produced. Some consumers prefer to pay more for products that are produced by "free range" animals, those that are allowed to graze freely outdoors. Free-range products are usually labeled in the supermarket. In many countries, laws govern the treatment of all farm animals and the way in which food is produced. Animal welfare groups, as well as concerned farmers, are always campaigning for improvements in the laws to protect animals as well as consumers.

▲ **Free-range chickens roam about naturally in the fresh air of the countryside.**

Guinea Pig on the Menu?

In North America and Europe, guinea pigs are much-loved family pets. We would never think of eating one! But in parts of South America, the guinea pig is a valued source of food. The guinea pig is from the Andes Mountains and it is a rodent, which means that it is related to mice and squirrels. The guinea pig was first domesticated for food as far back as five thousand years ago. Most families living in the Andes Mountains keep several guinea pigs in their home and feed them on vegetable scraps.

▲ **Guinea pigs take up much less room than larger livestock animals, such as cows or pigs, and they also reproduce more quickly.**

Chapter 4
The Hunters and Gatherers

All animals have a natural ability to find food, whether they prey on other animals or use a sharp sense of smell to search out plants. Humans discovered long ago that they could harness the abilities of certain animals to help in farming.

Hunters

The history of farming is closely connected to the history of animals. The ability of cats to hunt small animals has made them vital to farmers through the ages. Rats, mice, and birds could destroy a farmer's food supplies unless a cat, often called a mouser, stood guard. Mousers are still at work around the world today.

The first domesticated cats were probably naturally drawn to the role of mouser, for it guaranteed them food. Historians believe that the first wild

◀ **A pig helps its owner gather truffles, a delicate kind of fungus that grows underground and is highly valued for its flavor.**

▲ **Mousers have worked on farms for at least ten thousand years.**

Hunting for Food

For thousands of years, humans have relied on animals to help them hunt. Dogs traditionally have been the animal of choice. Humans have bred dogs with excellent hunting skills, such as a strong sense of smell and great speed.

Although people who hunt for their food are now rare, there are some tribes in Africa and Asia that still follow the old ways. For example, men of the Akepangi tribe of Papua New Guinea use dogs to find opossum and other small mammals in the rain forest.

While hunting for food is no longer commonly practiced, there are still many people who like to hunt for sport. All animal welfare organizations are against hunting for sport, whether it makes use of hounds to chase foxes or greyhounds to catch rabbits.

▲ Hunters from the Himba tribe and their dogs have killed a kudu, a type of antelope. Many Himba continue to lead a traditional way of life in the desert lands of northern Namibia, Africa.

▼ **Ferrets have been used by Europeans for hunting rabbits and rodents for at least two thousand years.**

cats were tamed at around the same time humans first began to settle and farm the land. This occurred about ten thousand years ago in an area that historians call the Fertile Crescent, which stretched from modern-day Turkey into Iraq and Israel.

Ferreting Them Out

Animals with hunting abilities are used to control all kinds of pests. In the United Kingdom and Australia, for example, rabbits are considered pests. In those countries, the way the rabbits feed can kill young trees and

"Many animal welfare groups are against ferreting, while ferreters say it is the kindest method of controlling the rabbit population."

destroy large areas of vegetation. Using ferrets is an age-old method of controlling the rabbit population.

With their slim build and brave nature, ferrets are pros at chasing rabbits and other small animals out of their burrows. The rabbits are then caught in a net by a human. Young and pregnant rabbits are let go, while older rabbits are quickly killed. Many animal welfare groups are against ferreting, while ferreters say it is the kindest method of controlling the rabbit population.

Some farmers use hunters to kill predators that attack their herds of sheep. Foxes have long been hunted for this reason. They have also been hunted as sport in many countries around the world. Using hound dogs and riding horses, people enjoyed chasing foxes. Today, animal welfare groups oppose foxhunting, believing it causes unnecessary suffering both to the foxes and the hounds. Fox-hunting as a sport is prohibited in some countries, and was outlawed in the United Kingdom in 2005.

Although hunting to control predators continues in farming communities around the world, some animals that were once considered pests are now protected to prevent their extinction, such as the wolf.

All Kinds of Gatherers

In many countries, humans have found ways to make use of the ability of some animals to gather food. The ideal situation is for the animal and human to work together for the benefit of both and without distress to the animal. In southern Thailand, for example, coconuts are grown on plantations. Using trained monkeys to scale the tall palm trees

◄ **Although a controversial sport, foxhunting still takes place in many countries around the world. These riders are taking part in a hunt in North Carolina.**

"When a fisherman sees that a cormorant has a large fish in its mouth, he brings it back to the boat where the cormorant spits it out."

is the easiest way for farmers to harvest the valuable fruit.

In parts of China and Japan, some traditional fishermen use trained cormorants to catch fish. The fishermen tie a string around a cormorant's throat, holding one end of the string to keep the bird under control. The loop around the bird's throat allows it to swallow only small fish. When a fisherman sees that a cormorant has a large fish in its mouth, he brings it back to the boat where the cormorant spits it out. A well-trained cormorant can feed an entire family. Today, though, most cormorant fishing is done only to entertain tourists.

◄ **A trained monkey gathers coconuts on a plantation in Thailand.**

▲ **Cormorants, known in China as** *lu-tse*, **are excellent fishers.**

Falconry

Falconry is a sport that uses trained birds of prey, such as falcons and hawks, to catch small animals. Birds of prey have keen eyes and sharp claws and beaks, which make them very skilled predators. Falconry is an ancient sport that may have started in China and Japan more than 2,500 years ago. It is thought to have spread to Europe by the fifth century CE. Since the eggs and chicks of birds of prey were always rare and expensive, falconry was a sport practiced by the wealthy. In fact, owning a trained falcon was a status symbol, which means that it was a sign of a person's power and money—just like owning a fast car or lots of jewelry is today. Today, although falconry is not illegal in most states, falconers must have a licence and pass a written test.

▲ **Strict laws protect wild birds of prey, so most birds used in falconry have been specially bred in captivity. Animal welfare organizations oppose the practise of falconry, as they do all hunting for sport.**

“The honeyguide's behavior is well known. The people of one tribe have even developed a special whistle to signal to the birds that they are ready to search for honey.”

In Africa, a bird called the Greater Honeyguide provides a useful service for humans by helping them find honey. These birds like to feed on the wax and larvae found in beehives. When a Greater Honeyguide wants to search for some wax, it signals to humans with a wavering call. The humans then follow the bird to the beehive. Once at the beehive, the human honey-hunters stun the bees with smoke and break open the hive.

▲ **A Greater Honeyguide knows the locations of many hives within its territory and can guide humans to them on demand.**

The bird can now eat its fill and the people can take home the honey. The honeyguide's behavior is well known. The people of one East African tribe have even developed a special whistle to signal to the birds that they are ready to search for honey.

Truffle Sniffing

Truffles are a kind of fungus that grows among the roots of certain trees, such as oaks, beeches, and poplars. Some truffles are edible and have a rich flavor that makes them highly prized by chefs. These delicious white and black truffles grow mainly in parts of southern and central Europe. The finest white truffles are hugely expensive – they can cost as much as $2,200 a pound!

Edible truffles develop underground and are found hidden beneath fallen

▲ **Female pigs have a natural ability to sniff out truffles. They also like to eat them!**

“*In recent years, truffle-hunters have trained dogs to find the little delicacies and dig them up without eating them.*”

leaves. They are often sniffed out by truffle pigs or trained truffle dogs. Truffle pigs have been used in Europe for centuries to search for truffles. All female pigs have a natural ability to smell truffles, as the fungus gives off a smell like a male pig, to which the females are attracted. The drawback of using pigs is that they are very eager to eat the truffles as soon as they find them! In recent years, truffle-hunters have trained dogs to find the little delicacies and dig them up without eating them. The dogs are rewarded for their work with treats such as biscuits.

▼ **This dog has been trained to sniff for truffles in Italy.**

The Right Dog for the Job

Over hundreds and even thousands of years, humans have developed different breeds of dog to perform different jobs. Even though most people would never dream of taking their dog hunting, many of today's popular pet breeds were developed for their special skills at hunting.

- The retrievers—These dogs were bred to retrieve, or collect, birds and other small animals that had been shot by hunters. Well-known retrievers include the golden retriever and the Labrador retriever. Retrievers are known for being gentle with their mouths, so that they do not damage the hunter's prize.

▲ **An English pointer shows its owner that it has spotted a bird in the long grass.**

▲ **Bloodhounds are valued for their ability to track people and animals by scent.**

- The pointers—Dogs such as the English pointer were bred to "point" out birds and small animals to the hunter. They did this by pointing their nose toward the animal.

- The spaniels—These small dogs were first bred to chase animals out of bushes and tall grasses, so that they could be captured by hunters. Breeds such as the King Charles spaniel and springer spaniel, with their long, floppy ears, make very popular house pets today.

- The hounds—Hounds are often divided into two groups: the sight hounds and the scent hounds. Sight hounds, such as the greyhound, are very fast and were bred to chase after prey by keeping it in sight. Scent hounds, such as the bloodhound, follow prey by tracking its scent.

Chapter 5
Career Guide

If you enjoy working with animals and love to be outdoors, a career in farming or ranching could be the right choice for you. You might also consider being a veterinarian or making a career in animal welfare.

Farmer

There are many different types of farming, including raising animals, growing crops, and managing orchards. Some farms combine various kinds of farming while others specialize in just one. Farmers own, or partly own, the land they use to raise animals or grow crops. Sometimes, a farm manager may run a farm or part of a farming business that is owned by someone else.

In the past, when farming was often a family business, the land was usually passed down from parent to child. Farming skills would be learned from the older generation. While this is still often the case today,

◄ **A groom walks a retired donkey at an animal sanctuary.**

▲ **A farmer and his granddaughter feed a lamb.**

" Cowboys and cowgirls feed the livestock, tend to injured animals, help transport animals, repair ranch fences and machinery, and perform other odd jobs. "

Do You Have What It Takes to Be a Farmer?

- Do you enjoy being with animals and have a strong interest in keeping them healthy and strong? (Remember that you will need to make difficult decisions and prevent yourself from getting too attached to your animals.)
- Are you interested in protecting the world's animals and plants—and their habitats—for the future?
- Would you be happy to work long days outdoors, whether it's raining or snowing?
- Do you enjoy managing a team of people?
- Do you have good business skills, from managing budgets and finding suitable buyers for your products to finding out about new farming methods?

anyone can choose to work in farming. Gaining experience by working on a farm is the most important step toward a farming career. Many farms offer on-the-job training. There are also a wide range of agricultural courses available at colleges and universities.

Cowboy or Cowgirl

Cowboys and cowgirls work on ranches, assisting with the raising of livestock. Although cowboys were made famous in movies about the Wild West, horse-riding farmhands can be found around the world.

Cowboys and cowgirls feed the livestock, tend to injured animals, help transport animals when needed, repair ranch fences and machinery, and perform other odd jobs. It is tough, demanding work that involves

▶ **A cowgirl wears leather leggings, called chaps, over her pants, which protect her legs while she works.**

being outdoors in all types of weather. No formal qualifications are needed to become a cowboy or cowgirl, although experience with horses and other animals is essential. The only way to become a cowboy or cowgirl is to find work on a ranch.

Veterinarian

A veterinarian, often called a vet, is a physician for animals. Many vets specialize in particular areas of animal care, such as taking care of livestock. Vets diagnose and treat health problems, vaccinate the animals against disease, and perform surgery. They also advise farmers and other animal owners about animal well-being. Some vets are employed by animal welfare organizations.

Gaining acceptance into a veterinary program is very competitive. After

More Careers in Animal Welfare

- Sanctuary worker—looking after retired, sick, or mistreated farm animals.
- Education officer—teaching people such as farmers and schoolchildren about animal welfare issues, both at home and abroad.
- Media campaigner—using the Internet, newspapers, television, and radio to inform the public about cases of animal cruelty and to campaign for changes in the law.

▲ **Neglected or unwanted farm animals can find safety in an animal sanctuary.**

graduating from high school, most students complete a four-year college program, earning a Bachelor of Science degree. Then they must be accepted into a veterinary program in order to become qualified vets. An alternative to becoming a veterinarian is to become a veterinary technician, which is similar to being an animal nurse. Veterinary technicians require a degree from either a two-year or a four-year college.

Animal Welfare Inspector

Animal welfare inspectors are employed by governments and

▲ **A vet advises a livestock farmer about feeding his herd.**

animal welfare organizations. They visit farms and other places where animals live to make sure that they are well fed, well housed, and well cared for. They advise farmers and other animal owners about animal care and the law. Wherever animals are found to be mistreated, inspectors gather evidence and report the owner to the authorities so that the person can be prosecuted.

Being an animal welfare inspector is a physically and emotionally demanding job. Good communication skills and an interest in the law are required. Some animal welfare organizations offer training for their inspectors, covering basic veterinary skills and animal welfare law. Other candidates usually require a college-level qualification in veterinary science, agriculture, or a related field.

▼ **Animal welfare workers rescue a dog from the floods in New Orleans after Hurricane Katrina struck in 2005.**

Glossary

breed
a group of animals within a species that share the same appearance

conservationists
people who work to protect the earth's resources

consumers
people who buy and use up things, such as products in a grocery store

domesticated
trained to live with or be used by human beings; tamed

fibers
long thin pieces of material, such as wool shorn from a sheep, which can be spun into thread that can then be woven into cloth

fleece
the coat of wool covering a sheep or other animal

hormones
chemicals made by certain glands in the body that help control growth, digestion, and other body processes

instinct
a way of acting or behaving that a person or animal is born with and does not have to learn

livestock
animals raised on a farm for the food or fiber they produce

predators
animals that hunt other animals for food

prey
an animal that is hunted by another animal for food

Further Information

BOOKS

Bowden, Rob. *Food and Farming (Sustainable World)*. San Diego: KidHaven Press, 2003.

Currie-McGhee, Leanne K. *Animal Rights (Overview Series)*. Farmington Hills, MI: Lucent Books, 2004.

Owen, Ruth. *Growing and Eating Green: Careers in Farming, Producing and Marketing Food.* New York: Crabtree Publishing Company, 2009.

Spilsbury, Louise. *Food and Agriculture: How We Use the Land*. Mankato, MN: Heinemann-Raintree, 2006.

Trumbauer, Lisa, *Exploring Animal Rights and Animal Welfare: Using Animals for Clothing*. Santa Barbara, CA: Greenwood Press, 2002.

Trumbauer, Lisa, E*xploring Animal Rights and Animal Welfare: Using Animals for Food*. Santa Barbara, CA: Greenwood Press, 2002.

WEBSITES

http://farmsanctuary.org

This organization's website has plenty of information about farm animal welfare and what the "humane" labels really mean on our meat, milk, and egg products.

www.fb.org

The website of the American Farm Bureau covers North America's largest organization of farmers and ranchers, offering farmers' views on various topics and concerns, as well as other useful information to help improve the lives of people living in rural communities.

http://library.thinkquest.org/TQ0312380/index.htm

A fun, interactive site, which includes games and puzzles related to farming.

www.museum.agropolis.fr/english/

The Agropolis Museum's site presents information about farming around the world and the history of agriculture.

www.nal.usda.gov/kids

The U. S. Department of Agriculture's page for schoolchildren offers information, links, and games covering various aspects of agriculture, farm animals, and related careers.

Index

PICTURE CREDITS
The photographs in this book are used by permission and through the courtesy of:

Corbis: 13 (Gallo Images/Martin Harvey), 15 (Jim Zuckerman), 16 (DLILLC), 18 (Kit Houghton), 26 (Franz-Marc Frei), 29 (E Simanor/Robert Harding World Imagery), 30 (Ashley Cooper), 34 (Richard A. Cooke), 39 (Anne Hodalic), 40 (Owen Franken), 42 (Peter Johnson), 44 (Will and Deni McIntyre), 49 (Nigel J. Dennis/Gallo Images), 50 (Yves Gellie), 51 (Owen Franken), 55 (Ariel Skelley)

Dreamstime: 2 (Starharper), 6 (Lee Torrens), 9 (Cynoclub), 12 (Mike Rogal), 20, 47 (Christophe Testi)

FLPA: 23 (John Watkins), 41 (Erica Olsen), 43 (Martin H. Smith)

Fotolia: 11 (RbbrDckyBK), 24 (Josef M. Ilek), 25 (Clement Billet), 28 (Filipebvarela), 32 bottom (Jiew Wan Tan), 46 (TMAX), 48 (Grzegorz Wolczyk), 57 (Jeanne Hatch), 58 right (Monkey Business Images)

Getty Images: 7 (Stuart and Michele Westmorland), 54 (Matt Cardy), 58 left (Matt Cardy)

iStockphoto: 8 (Klaas Lingbeek-van Kranen), 10 (Yuriy Sukhovenko), 17 (Cynthia Baldauf), 27 (Anantha Vardhan), 31 (Sean Wallace Jones), 33 (Esemelwe), 36 (Marcelo Silva), 38 (Ed Westmacott), 53 (Mike Dabell)

Photos.com: 19, 52

Photoshot: 21 (Bryan and Cherry Alexander), 37 (Eltan Simanor/UPPA), 59 (Carrie Pratt/St. Petersburg Times/WpN)

Wikimedia Creative Commons Licence: 22 (Ralf Roletschek), 32 top (Fastily)

ABOUT THE AUTHOR
Claudia Martin is an author and editor with many years of experience creating books for children about the natural world, society, and history. She has a keen interest in animals and their relationship with humans. Her most recent books about animals include *Picking Your Pet* and *The Big Book of Questions and Answers*.